Relationship DETOX

Praise for Relationship DETOX

"Great book! Often, books written about relationships fall into two categories—too personal or too academic. Not this book. It is written from the heart, but not in a way that is overwhelming. It is practical, with examples to help the reader gain further insight. Jodi's FORWARD method is simple but effective—it is a game-changer!"

—**David Lawson**, Relationship Counselor
and Coach, Finding the Light

"I bet most people know someone who hasn't found the love of their life and has fallen into frustration and discontent over their future prospects, not wanting to be alone but not knowing how to find that special partner either. *Relationship Detox* gives them the tools to reset their dating life and move forward with focus and integrity."

—**Carrie Saynisch**, Health and Wellness Coach

"If we're incredibly fortunate, we've found our mate and are happy for the rest of our lives—growing and changing together—embracing our similarities and our differences. But the odds are stacked against us. *Unless* we have a process such as the one Jodi lays out for us here. Jodi shows her vulnerability, ensuring us that we're not the only ones with flaws. She talks to us in this book like a wiser, non-judgmental friend, and she guides us—in plain language—to ask ourselves the big questions that will lead to our authentic selves. She coaches us to understand ourselves better so that we can connect with a partner who loves us, supports us, challenges us, and helps us become all we ever wanted to be and more."

–Karen Cain, Realtor

"Just over a year ago, my 22-year toxic relationship exploded. Deep down, I knew that day would come, yet I was unprepared for the depth of my loss of self-worth and feelings of personal failure. The last months have been filled with searching for a path to right my battered soul. At last, here it is! Your proposal of FORWARD action has a relatable framework destined for confident success. Your book and concept are engaging, accessible, and empowering. Thank you for assisting me in finding a new today and tomorrow."

–Holly Levison

"Breaking old patterns requires strategy and heart. Jodi's FORWARD Framework provides gentle guidance, encouraging you to be kind to yourself as you walk through the challenging, yet rewarding, path to take back your power. Do the work, make the changes, embrace the new you, and prosper!"

–Kim Schierl

"What an amazing book! I was able to relate to looking back at past relationships and the types of men I have been drawn to, and, most of all, how I allowed those people to control my life. After reading *Relationship Detox*, I am on a new journey. Thank you, Jodi for writing this and helping me along my new path!"

–Suzette Plemel, LMT

Relationship
DETOX

*7 Steps to Prepare for
Your Ideal Relationship*

Jodi Schuelke

NEW YORK

NASHVILLE • MELBOURNE • VANCOUVER

Relationship DETOX
7 Steps to Prepare for Your Ideal Relationship

Published in New York, New York, by Morgan James Publishing in partnership with Difference Press. Morgan James is a trademark of Morgan James, LLC. www.MorganJamesPublishing.com

The Morgan James Speakers Group can bring authors to your live event. For more information or to book an event visit The Morgan James Speakers Group at www.TheMorganJamesSpeakersGroup.com.

ISBN 978-1-68350-539-6 paperback
ISBN 978-1-68350-540-2 eBook
Library of Congress Control Number: 2017905648

Cover Design by:
Rachel Lopez
www.r2cdesign.com

Interior Design by:
Bonnie Bushman
The Whole Caboodle Graphic Design

In an effort to support local communities, raise awareness and funds, Morgan James Publishing donates a percentage of all book sales for the life of each book to Habitat for Humanity Peninsula and Greater Williamsburg.

Get involved today! Visit
www.MorganJamesBuilds.com

Dedication

To Dawn, for lighting the pathway
for me to step into my future self.

Table of Contents

Introduction

If you've picked up this book, it's my hunch you're feeling exhausted from the whole dating scene and busting your butt trying to find *your* Mr. Wonderful and finally feel happy. You've longed to be treated like a lady, to feel respected and appreciated, to feel loved and accepted for who you are. Instead, you've tried to mold yourself to others' expectations, to get noticed or retain their attention.

You've expended lots of time and energy getting to know each new guy and being overly empathetic to his story and current circumstances. You stepped in to help him out in different ways—cleaned his apartment, showed him how to be more organized or manage his money better, loaned him money, footed the bill for dinner and a movie when he's the one who asked you out, volunteered to be the designated driver so you could be a part of *his* night out with *his* friends. Or maybe you've stepped in to help care for his kids or chauffeur them around. You've even made excuses for his poor behavior and tried to teach him how to be in a relationship, in hopes that he'd come around and ideally become that guy you've always dreamed about.

Or maybe you've talked to your friends or family, surveying them for ideas on how to change (a.k.a. "fix") things with this guy. As you've implemented their "helpful" suggestions, you've continued to hope the person you set your sights on will finally "come around."

But, as more time goes by with no significant or consistent changes, you find yourself feeling more and more frustrated. You recognize what you've done, but you don't know how to stop these behaviors of yours.

You've been waiting for the right guy to come along. You've believed it was up to him to come in and sweep you off your feet and rescue you. So you busied yourself with searching and chasing, while ignoring your intuition and allowing yourself to fall prey to relationships that would fit, but only if you molded him just right. Or that started out promising and then, a short time later, devolved into something else—something emotionally draining, toxic, or just plain icky.

You chose to do all of that because you're looking for a safety net.

I know you're feeling stressed. This really sucks. You're not feeling good about yourself and now you're starting to feel bitter toward men. You want to be happy, have a decent relationship, and finally feel settled; but no matter what you try, it doesn't seem to work. You can't understand why you keep falling into the same rut and repeating the same patterns, dating the same type of guy.

What you do know is that you want it to stop.

Meet Jenna

Jenna is a college-educated career woman and the single mother of two young teenagers. She lives in the suburbs a short commute from her corporate IT job. Jenna was married once before, to her children's father, but the marriage quickly fell apart following the realization that they only got married and stayed married because of the kids.

When I met Jenna, she had been divorced for about eight years. During that time she'd had a variety of relationships—a long-term rebound relationship after her divorce, followed by a string of short-term and casual relationships. In between those, she continued to date and kept her profile active on a variety of dating sites and apps.

In addition to using online dating, Jenna also built a circle of single friends—gals and guys—who she met up with at dance clubs or bars to hang out with and have fun whenever she didn't have a date. After a few cocktails, Jenna's inhibitions decreased and she'd soon be off flirting and dancing with random attractive men. On a few occasions—typically following a recent break-up—she'd take a man home for the night.

Outside of the club scene, Jenna made sure that when she was out running errands, grocery shopping, or attending her kids' activities she was always fashionably dressed, with her hair and make-up done. She knew how to assess the environment and quickly spot potential single men, as well as how to carry herself to get noticed. Despite all of her efforts, Jenna never met a potential date that way.

Although Jenna found it relatively easy to garner attention online or in the clubs, she began to see that the quality of men she attracted that way weren't really very good for her. Most of the men she dated had some type of addiction (mainly alcohol), were commitment-phobes, narcissists, only interested in a convenient booty call, or were actually married and pretending to be single. The few men she met who weren't like that—who treated her respectfully and tried to *court* her—totally freaked her out and she quickly dumped them, claiming they were weird or had too many quirks.

To outsiders, Jenna appeared to be happy, to have her life under control, and to be content with being single. On the inside, she felt like her love life was an absolute mess! She was ashamed that she'd been single for so long, and even worried that her kids, married friends, and family thought there was something wrong with her because none of her relationships ever really stuck.

The tipping point for Jenna was when she began to notice her married friends referencing her dates as "your latest fling" or "the flavor of the week." Those comments got Jenna's attention and caused her to question what the hell she'd been doing.

When Jenna was finally able to admit that she didn't want to live that way any longer and was ready to do something about it, everything began to shift.

The Cost of Staying on That Path

As we see from Jenna's story, the obvious cost of continuing those same dating patterns was her true happiness. In addition, her lifestyle was affecting her relationships with her kids, friends, and even family. Her desperation to continue to date unfit men just so she didn't feel alone, and her tendencies toward behaving in a more and more risqué way, resulted in increasingly negative perceptions of her by her loved ones. Jenna also began to see how her desperate dating lifestyle didn't really jibe with the lifestyles of her married or coupled friends.

What she never told those friends was that she desperately wanted a life like theirs—one where she had someone to count on, who truly loved her, and who wanted to share and build a life together.

The Benefits of Changing Course

Choosing to step away from the life you've known for so long and set a course for a different direction will be the beginning of a beautiful transformation for you. This is a gift to yourself.

Imagine a life where you feel free to be fully yourself. You start anew. You spend your free time doing things you enjoy, and you are more mentally present for your kids and loved ones. You are able to pursue goals and dreams you'd put on the backburner. Gone are the days of searching, chasing, and shape-shifting yourself to fit a man's preferences or fantasies, because you don't need to do that anymore—it doesn't matter anymore. You can get what you need without doing that. You can breathe easily.

Life is so much better when your only regret is that you didn't make this change years sooner!

But You're Afraid

I understand that you may be feeling that you did something wrong to have allowed this lifestyle to go on for so long. You may have doubts that you will ever meet a decent guy, and maybe you even feel like you don't deserve that. You may worry that your single friends might think you're abandoning them if you stop hanging out in the club scene. You may think your loved ones won't believe you'll follow through on making real changes, because any previous attempts to break these patterns left you feeling lonely and depressed, which resulted in you sliding backwards and settling for unavailable men again. You may even have a sick feeling in your stomach from worrying about how to step away from this life you've known for so long. You don't know where to even start with making a different life for yourself.

Sweetheart, I totally get it. I know the frustration and pain of falling back into that rut. I understand where you've been, because I've been there too.

What you've experienced is not all your fault. You're absolutely not crazy, needy, a train wreck, trashy, or a whore. Other people may have said those mean things, but they don't get a say. There's nothing wrong with wanting a healthy relationship, wanting to settle down, or wanting to have a happy life.

Fear is a natural, protective instinct and it comes in when we are drawn toward making a change, especially if it's an important one. Fear is intended to keep us safe, but when you hide behind fear versus utilizing it as a catalyst for change, you'll stay stuck in the same patterns and continue to feel miserable. My dear, what you want is important. You are smart, and you *can* do this. I can help.

I Will Show You the Way

This book chronicles the journey I went on after my divorce, when I went from rebounding, jumping into my *30s Gone Wild* phase, getting my life together, and finally to finding the relationship of my dreams and getting married again. Mistakes and missteps I experienced along the way are also shared, which I hope will show you that you are not alone and will help you to better navigate the process so you can quickly transform your life.

I've included case studies about clients I've coached, as well as insights from mental health professionals.

My intention is that this book helps you cross over to a better and healthier love life, and a more promising future for yourself and your children.

The Road Ahead

We're going to explore the seven steps of the FORWARD Framework process. These steps have been strategically designed to help you take your love life to the next level. Through the course of this book, I walk you through the exact steps I took when I went through my own relationship detox, and that I help my clients successfully use. I'll share the concepts and strategies that took me years to develop and learn—including mistakes I made and tactics I used to keep me on track—so that you can shorten your journey.

Each of the seven FORWARD Framework steps is designed to take you through a mapped-out plan for successfully completing your relationship detox and setting you up to find your ideal relationship.

As you read through this book, I invite you to trust the process.

Chapter 1

My Story

I n my first book, *I Just Want Out*, I shared the story of my first marriage and the steps I took to leave my emotionally abusive husband and remove that daily toxicity from my and my children's lives. This book picks up shortly after I left my first marriage and continues through the next ten years, up to meeting the man who would become my second, current, wonderful husband.

The Rebound

Upon leaving my emotionally abusive first marriage, I set my sights on creating a brand new life for myself and my kids.

What I hadn't anticipated was being completely vulnerable and naïve. Along comes Mr. Rebound, an old high school friend of my older brother, someone I had known for years, too. He was nice and fun to be around. A few weeks after my divorce, I found myself out on a date with Mr. Rebound, thoroughly enjoying the attention and being treated so respectfully. It was refreshing.

It didn't take long for our friendship to warp into a serious romance. Mr. Rebound lived a few hours away and, after a year of dating, he took a job closer to me and moved in with me. The first six months of living together felt like a honeymoon—he had swooped in and rescued me when I was vulnerable—and I couldn't remember ever being happier. Until, that is, reality crept in and the *real* man-child surfaced.

Mr. Rebound stopped financially contributing to the household bills and neglected household chores, deciding to, instead, zone out all weekend in front of the TV. He complained to his friends about our relationship, but pretended to me that all was fine. He consistently lied about his smoking addiction, even when confronted, and continued to have "friendships" with his exes, despite his promise not to do so anymore. He even bought flowers and romantic cards and offered me false promises to never do such things again, trying to make amends after arguments, only to then do it again and again. My kids struggled with the changes in his demeanor and began acting out in different ways, to the point where I found myself consistently thrust in the middle of fights over petty issues and getting in protective mother-bear mode.

Fast forward a couple of years and I was calling off our engagement, canceling wedding plans, forfeiting down payments, and Mr. Rebound was signing over the deed to the house we had bought together the year before. Our infatuation had turned tumultuous and toxic and I was ready to be rid of all the drama and stress that came from being in a relationship with a man-child.

We moved him out, and I set my sights on moving on with my life.

Online Dating Newbie

After the dust settled from that break-up, I decided to try online dating to see what that was like. I signed up for Match.com, created my profile, and started meeting some men and having conversations. I wasn't really sure what I was looking for, but knew the next guy couldn't be *anything* like my ex-husband or Mr. Rebound. Soon I was chatting online, then talking on the phone with a few different guys, and finally I started going out on dates. Many of the guys were nice, and I enjoyed the conversations and their company, but I found that some were more interested in me than I was in them.

Back-to-Back Boyfriends

After a few months of casual dating, I stepped into a series of relationships with different men, for spans ranging from a month to six months. That went on for over six years and, trickled throughout, were the *real* life lessons. There was the narcissist I dated twice. There were two alcoholics. There were a few commitment-phobes, and there was the corporate traveler who was only available on Saturday nights.

In the earlier relationships, I worked hard to keep them moving forward by suggesting or making plans for us to do fun activities together. I would also help them out whenever I could, making their needs a priority over mine and even over my kids'. When the relationship started to fall apart, I'd do everything I could to fix things, even if that meant trying to change who *I* was. But that act never lasted long, because I couldn't fake it, and they had lost interest.

Maybe you know what it's like to have your heart broken, or even to break someone else's heart. Hopefully, most of your relationships have ended respectfully and you were able to remain friends afterwards. That was often the case with me, when the men I had dated were reasonably healthy. But there were two men I dated, at different times, during this phase—John and Kyle, better known as "The Toxic Two."

I had the unfortunate experience of breaking John's heart. I have been on both sides of that so I understood that he was upset, but when he showed up unexpectedly at my place of work bearing flowers and begging me to go to lunch with him, sent me love letters in the mail multiple times a week, and repeatedly drove past my house at night, I knew I had to cut off the relationship completely. We could *not* stay friends. With Kyle, it was harder, because I genuinely wanted to stay friends with his daughters, but the truth was I knew he was toxic and cutting him off meant cutting off the whole family.

Hopefully, that type of situation will be rare for you. But when toxic people come into your life, you need to make sure you have the tools to get them out. This can be trickier than it looks!

How I Figured It Out

What I didn't openly share with my dates during that six-year dating frenzy was how miserable and lonely I was on the inside. I had been to therapy off and on, and had read countless self-help books, magazine articles, and blog posts on how to land your dream guy. I'd even watched all the *happily ever after* romantic comedy movies. As time went on and I continued to explore all the different dating strategies—how to be sexier, smarter, skinnier, conservative, and uncommitted yet still be soft and willing to surrender—it felt all wrong. I found myself getting angry and fed up with trying to do all the work and chasing guys hoping *they'd* accept *me*.

What finally occurred to me was that everything I had been doing was going against nature. I was chasing the male and he was deciding if I was acceptable. My self-worth seemed to be based on whether I was worthy enough for him.

In nature, it's the complete opposite—the male pursues the female and *she* decides. That realization led me to start doing some intense research. None of the books I found that were written by therapists or PhDs about what I shouldn't do—no rebounds, no dating for at least a year after your divorce, yadda-yadda—told me *how* to step off the crazy dating train I was on and reset my life in a way that would rid the icky people from it and stop me from making unhealthy choices, or told me how get swift and lasting results.

So, I set out to figure it out on my own.

The FORWARD Framework™

What I learned by leaving my old life behind and taking steps to break free of poor dating patterns and habits isn't for the weak-hearted, but it was absolutely worth it. I had to step into my power, fully embrace it, and work hard. I had a responsibility to myself as an intelligent woman and as a mother to model healthy behavior and choices to my two sons. I was willing to take the necessary steps and potential risks to give us a better future. And that's exactly what I want for you: a better future.

I've pooled all my experience and trial-and-error efforts, research, and my clients' experiences, as well as insights from relationship experts, into a seven-step process I call the FORWARD Framework. It's what I wish I'd had years ago to guide me through transforming my life faster, so it would've been easier and wouldn't have taken so long to find my wonderful second husband.

The following chapters will walk you through each of the steps of The FORWARD Framework, including to-dos, how-tos, what to avoid, and why the steps are important. Based on your personal situation, you can select the things to do that work best for you.

The FORWARD Framework is an easy-to-follow guide intended to help you successfully complete your relationship detox. It can help you better prepare, based on your personal situation, for a better relationship, and also help you keep your wits about you while you're going through the transformational process.

Plus, I will be right here in this book walking alongside you throughout your journey. You can trust that this process will help you reach your goal of detoxing from unhealthy relationships and patterns so that you can finally find your ideal relationship. This process can help you open up space so you can create the life you've always dreamed about.

FORWARD Framework™ Steps

F = Focus Your Attention—The first step is about how to get started on becoming your own safety net, including strategy and self-love, embracing being single, making the commitment, setting a date, and being all-in.

O = Opting Out of Past Habits—The second step goes into detail about letting go of the old you, shedding excessive baggage, building a healthy support network, initial fears you may be experiencing, and taking back your power.

R = Reflect Back—In step three, we take a look at your relationship history and identify their pros and cons.

W = Wake up to Your Own Wisdom—The next step is about connecting to your inner-wisdom. You'll begin to formulate your future life and what you truly want your ideal relationship to look like, as well as learn how to become the future you by tuning in to yourself, journaling, and increasing your self-care.

A = Take Action—Doing the previous steps allows you to then create a game plan to best fit your situation. We'll touch on creating structure, incorporating healthy transformative alternatives into your daily routine, and fully stepping into the future you.

R = Raise Your Resilience—It's important that you're prepared for potential challenges. Not everything will go perfectly, nor will everyone be supportive of your changes. This step helps you identify potential drama as well as learn how to be resilient when faced with challenges or drama along the way.

D = Dedicate Yourself to Your Success—The final step is staying true to reaching your goal of completing your relationship detox. You'll learn how to maintain your momentum, keep from slipping backward, lay out your game plan, establish boundaries, and change your language to match your growing self-confidence.

What to Expect Along the Journey

As you read through the following chapters you may have bouts of fear or self-doubt. You will be learning new concepts, methods, and things you may have never considered. Some information may challenge you in ways that scare you; they may even make you angry and want to give up, because it's hard work. Please be kind to yourself and remember that getting rid of the impurities from your life, embarking on a new beginning, and rewriting your relationship future can feel nerve-wracking.

This is completely normal.

I invite you to first take some time to evaluate where you are now and whether you're ready to step forward. Use those moments to envision the life and relationship you want, so that you'll have a touchstone, a reason for going through the FORWARD Framework Process.

When you're done, check back in with yourself to see how you feel and then get started with the steps in earnest.

Consider this book your guide for creating a new and better life for yourself.

Read on to discover the way forward.

Chapter 2

Step 1: Focus Your Attention

Having a healthy and fulfilling relationship with a partner is wonderful, and is what I believe everyone truly wants deep down. But in order to have that with a partner, one must first have a healthy relationship with oneself.

Doing a relationship detox is about focusing your attention on expanding and filling yourself with the right stuff—the right mindset, concepts, activities, and people. When you do so, there won't be any room left for unhealthy choices and unwanted drama.

The FORWARD Framework process is a surefire way to create changes and shifts in your perception that will lay a new foundation and bring lasting results.

Become Your Own Safety Net

Your childhood and upbringing, and cultural or religious beliefs, can have a big influence on how you view relationships. You may believe there's safety in partnership and that you *need* the other person to make you feel happy.

One of the hardest, yet most liberating, concepts I learned was that I did *not* need a man to fill the void I felt inside or to make me feel whole. I had to let go of those beliefs and begin to trust in myself and rely on myself, not outsiders, in order to get what I needed.

Learning how to rely on yourself and become your own safety net will cultivate the confidence you need to finally change those ingrained habits. It's easier to let go of the concept of what you *thought* was your safety net when you realize it was only an illusion. Letting go of those old beliefs and replacing them with new ways of thinking will open you up to new and exciting opportunities.

Although it doesn't happen overnight, when you accept that you are your own safety net, letting go of unhealthy choices will become a reality much sooner.

In the upcoming sections we'll look at how to get you there by ridding the disruptive, unwanted, and harmful people and situations from your life.

It Takes Strategy and Heart

There's a lot that goes into changing old habits and thinking patterns—and it requires both strategy *and* heart. *Strategy* is the structure and tactics, and *heart* is your mindset and intuition. You'll have to learn to walk *both* paths—understanding the concepts and parameters, but also keeping a compassionate eye out for ways you might tend to sabotage yourself.

This book takes you through the planning and practicing of the strategies, and we wrap up with you owning the new you—the person you've become. All of it is designed to help you implement the concepts in such a way that they become second nature.

You're not going to find your own sense of balance, however, until you actually go through the FORWARD

Framework process. There will, most likely, be challenges, but I'm certain there will be many more victories.

You may want to skim through and try to cherry-pick and implement only some of the parts of the process, but I guarantee you it won't work. The way to change your relationship future is to fully step into the relationship detox process and make it happen. It may be scary, but it's absolutely worth it –that's the value of completing it.

This, my friend, is going to transform your life!

Embrace Being Single

Yes, you read that right—it's time to fully embrace singlehood. What this specifically means is that you take a hiatus from dating for a while. No need to panic—all of my clients who've gone on to finding their ideal relationship first committed to taking a hiatus, and they have said it was the *best* decision they made.

Now, I realize you might have some hesitation about this, because there's a stigma in society about being okay with being single and not wanting to date. Outsiders may wonder if there's something wrong with you or tease that you'll become a "crazy cat lady." Maybe you've even tried going the single route for a while, but found yourself feeling utterly lonely and unsure about what to do with your extra free time. After a point, you just gave up and put yourself back out there, only to find yourself falling for the same unhealthy guys again.

Embracing being single doesn't mean your life is over or that this is a forever arrangement. Much to the contrary, it's an exciting new way to live that helps you see more clearly all the unhealthy habits, patterns, and people that have kept you feeling stuck and unhappy. It's a way of life that enables you to also embrace who you are, focus on what you're doing, and get clear about what you really want. It sets you up to find your ideal relationship sooner.

Embracing being single is an opportunity for you to learn about yourself through exploration and to reprioritize your life around what you've discovered that's in alignment with your own dreams and goals.

In with Both Feet

Before we continue, I want to address an all too common challenge I've seen over the years: only having one foot in and not being fully committed to this process. Now's the time to get super honest with yourself about what you've done in the past or might be tempted to do.

In the past you may have declared in a state of frustration that you were done with men and dating. But, in reality, you were still in "looking mode," doing things like continuously checking your online dating accounts or apps, or jumping onto social media and engaging in flirtatious conversations when you were bored. Maybe you went on secret dates and didn't even tell your best girlfriend, for fear she'd call you out on it. Or you rationalized to yourself that it wasn't really a date because you went "dutch."

Maybe you're *still* hanging onto that going-nowhere relationship because you think by staying friends and casually hanging out and keeping yourself in the picture you're making progress in getting him to *finally* come around. You say you're okay with it being a casual thing or an open relationship, but all the while inside you feel let down and unlovable. If you don't hear from him, you stalk his whereabouts on social media, send him angry or drunk texts, or even give ultimatums that end up blowing up in your face.

Time and again, all of that exhausting work, time, and energy (and probably money, too) that you've wasted trying to make a guy finally see you, and to keep him happy, and to hopefully bring the two of you two closer ultimately ends in you feeling disappointed and miserable. That doesn't sound freeing and transformative one bit.

The honest-to-God's truth is, if you're in "looking mode" or still "hanging on," you are not embracing being single.

Step 1 Tool—Cleanse Commitment

To get started, make a pledge to cease *all* active *and* passive dating activities for a minimum of eight weeks, but twelve weeks is ideal. Yes, my dear, it's time to turn off the "man-tap" and take some quality time to be alone with you. This commitment is about being able to confidently say, "Who am I to be dating anyone right now until I've got my life figured out?"

To help you stay true to yourself and prevent yourself from slipping backwards, online dating accounts or apps should be closed or profiles deactivated—you can re-activate them at a future date if you want to then. With social media, your relationship status should not be displayed at all and, if your personal Facebook account is public, go ahead and change access to "friends only." You will also want to remove yourself from or turn off notifications for any dating groups you may have been participating in.

These initial changes will reduce the chances of you getting distracted from your goal.

This dating break is a surefire way to do a successful relationship detox, rid yourself of the unhealthy habits, and get you unstuck from the rut you find yourself in. It will also help you cultivate more confidence, so you can continue to move forward faster toward your goal of being in your ideal relationship.

If you are fortunate to have supportive loved ones who want to see you succeed, feel free to recruit them to help you stay accountable over the course of the FORWARD Framework process.

Please be kind to yourself as you consider the best ways to handle the Cleanse Commitment and as you grow into a greater position of strength and readiness. It may seem difficult to stay true to the agreement and wait for the cleanse and detox to be completed in reality, but part of what's happening as you wait is that you are becoming a person capable of taking care of yourself and putting yourself as a priority.

Picking a Start Date

What makes this more real is putting your Cleanse Commitment start date in your calendar. But don't make it start in, like, six months from now. Make it soon enough so the material in this book is still fresh in your mind.

This is where things get real, really quick.

There's never a perfect start date. But if you find yourself floundering or worrying about upcoming social activities, the holidays, vacations, or whatever—know that that's just your fear getting in the way and trying to create a delay. Also, be careful not to allow obsessing about the fine details or worrying about what others might think take over your process. Your intention is much more powerful than your fear.

Ask yourself this: *Who do I want to be at the end of my relationship detox?*

Do you want to *still* feel frustrated and scared? Lonely and angry? Spinning your wheels trying to convince a man to love you and treat you the way you deserve?

Or do you want to feel different? Clearer? More confident? Less dependent or needy? Lighter from letting go of the old ways of thinking? Free from having to worry about a guy's emotional baggage?

I have a hunch it's the latter paragraph. So pick your day, put it in your calendar, and anchor to it!

♥ ♥ ♥

Focusing your attention in this way will help to lay the necessary foundation and prepare you to successfully complete your Relationship Detox. The next chapter will help you move forward in establishing the outcome you want to achieve.

Chapter 3

Step 2: Opting Out of Past Habits

A successful relationship detox entails knowing what outcome you want for yourself. This step can be done in conjunction with Step 1 as you do the Cleanse Commitment. Deciding to hop out of the dating arena after your last break-up was a noble decision, but I have a hunch you might be feeling a little freaked out. You are starting to change. Doing this relationship detox *will* thrust you forward into being able to stand on your own and deal with who you are—possibly for the very first time.

The FORWARD Framework process enables you to determine who you are, who you want to be, and then how to become it. You'll connect with your personal values and be able to see more clearly what you want your life to look like. Once you know who you *really* are, you can take the next steps that help you find your ideal relationship.

This is an opportunity for you to connect (or reconnect) with yourself as an independent woman. Knowing what outcome you want for yourself also means having the courage to let go of anyone not healthy for you, or anything that seems to want to be taken from you, such as the bad influencers or those who do not respect your wishes and dreams. Doing so enables you to better assess where to go from here.

Saying Good-Bye to the Old You

When you're in a relationship with a man who is emotionally unavailable, it's easy to display *needy* behaviors, because he's not giving you what you really want, which is partnership, openness, and vulnerability. As women, when we don't get what we want, we tend to try harder, attempting to bring him closer by making him the center of our world, or trying to teach him "how to be" in a relationship.

In my client Valerie's experience, the result was that when she asked for more from an unavailable man, she'd get a bit of effort for a short time, but then he would revert back to how he had been. She heard from countless men that she was being too needy, or too clingy, or too smothering. Valerie could see *some* truth in what they said, but hearing it still stung.

There's a spectrum of neediness, from extreme codependency to the healthier end, where you simply need another person's help. The more men you've been involved with who are emotionally unavailable and not the right fit, the more codependent behaviors occur.

Depending on your relationship history, you may have fallen anywhere on that spectrum at one time or another. What I want you to know is that it's okay! What's important to focus on now is letting go of those needy *habits*. This happens by putting yourself at the source and practicing only needing yourself rather than having to be in a relationship. A man should be like an accessory to your life—he makes it better (more on that later) but isn't everything.

Shedding Excessive Baggage

In the Introduction, I shared Jenna's story with you. Part of establishing her outcome included looking at her circle of influence—her family, friends, coworkers, and, more specifically, the singles group she frequented the clubs with.

Although Jenna loved her single-friends group, she could also see that they, too, had not been making the wisest choices when it came to dating. They were very caught up in the club scene and all the superficial drama that came with partying a lot. Thanks in part to her kids having lots of sports and extra-curricular activities, Jenna had a legitimate excuse for passing on the invites. As her Focus weeks passed and she got into her Cleanse Commitment, Jenna noticed that she really didn't miss going out with her friends, even when they called her the next day to brag about their promiscuous activities.

If you want to make significant changes in your life, especially when it comes to getting serious about finding your ideal relationship, the people you take up company with also have to be taken into consideration and evaluated. Your peers can have a negative impact on your relationship detox progress. They may even sabotage your efforts, because they're not ready (or interested) in cleaning up their own lives or finding lasting partners. They may consider it more fun to have single friends while they're still single.

In Jenna's situation, she slowly stepped away from going out to the clubs with her single friends and instead met them randomly for weekday lunches. That enabled them to still stay connected, but for limited amounts of time and in a less-triggering environment.

Shedding excessive baggage can also pertain to people in your life such as family or coworkers. Based on your experiences when interacting with those individuals, decide where to draw the line.

Build Your Support Network

In an earlier chapter, I suggested that you reach out to supportive friends or loved ones to help yourself stay on track during your relationship detox. They can be any people—single or married—with whom you have a mutual respect. Surrounding yourself with people you trust and who want only the best for you is an important step in this process. You'll benefit from having support along the way, and even nudging or reassurance if you find yourself slipping. Your support network is a great way to expand your friendship circle, and can offer you new and interesting people to hang out with when you don't have other plans or are feeling lonely and want some company.

What seems to make the greatest difference when you approach individuals in your support network is how you choose to speak to them. Approaching them in a calm and confident manner, stating your decision to step away from dating for awhile, versus bringing in drama or acting like a martyr, will help them see how serious you are about making positive changes in your life. Having your game plan thought through, sharing what you've learned so far, and simply asking for their moral support is a great strategy. I have a hunch that what you'll get in return will be so much more than just having someone to lean on for support. It's also an opportunity to have deeper and more meaningful friendships.

Be careful not to rely too heavily on your support network and expect them to hold your hand through every single instance or moment of fear or uncertainty. Doing so can put a strain on even your most supportive friends or loved ones. A core ingredient of your relationship detox is learning and practicing the art of being able to rely on yourself, to a degree, when faced with fear.

Facing Fear

As you step through the FORWARD Framework process, I suspect you'll experience feelings of uncertainty or fear of loneliness, despite having expanded your support network.

Or, after some time of being focused on yourself, some "blast from the past" will re-emerge and try to coax you to get together or want to engage in titillating phone conversations, texting, or online chats. If that happens, I invite you to simply not engage in any type of conversation. If need be, go through the contacts in your phone and relabel those names as, for example, "Do Not Answer-Doug," or completely block them from being able to contact you.

Whatever pops up, know that you may be faced with enticing options, hear nagging voices in your head saying, *What's one drink? It's innocent. It'll be fine.* You're going to need to ignore that or any other sabotage distractions and step right into the face of fear—stand toe to toe with it and acknowledge that, even though you might be feeling lonely or bored, you're not going to allow that to knock you off track and implode your forward momentum and progress. *That*, my dear, is true strength. You *are* stronger than loneliness and fear. Use any fear that comes up to fuel your continued *forward* progress.

Step 2 Tool—Take Back Your Power

Taking back your power is a self-awareness technique. It's the practice of pulling back your power from the places it can try to run off to without your consent. Your power is comprised of your attention, things you haven't completed (e.g., that list of to-dos), things you put up with or refuse to tolerate, as well as the language you use.

Many people give away their power by splitting their attention in a hundred different directions. Women, in particular, are prone to multitasking and trying to juggle multiple things at once, falsely thinking that equates to a higher level of success.

Giving away power can also take the form of those thoughts that become worries that veer your attention into a downward spiral. Or thoughts that falsely feel good in the moment, but are actually taking you off course from your Cleanse Commitment.

Taking back your power can be as simple as reflecting back on each day to see where your attention and energy were spent. At the end of each day, take some quiet time to review the day and ask yourself these three questions:

- How did I spend my energy and attention today?
- What parts of this day gave me energy?
- What am I looking forward to about tomorrow?

Learning to take back your power is an amazing skill set you can master. When that starts to happen, you begin to understand the sheer power of your attention.

Becoming more aware of your thoughts and actions is a key piece of your relationship detox journey.

In the next chapter we'll look back on your relationship history.

Chapter 4

Step 3: Reflect Back

Mark pushed his chair back from the table and slid the check toward Carrie. She grabbed the bill and looked at it. *$150 for a crappy dinner with a massive jerk*, she thought, *Guess I'll only be able to make the minimum payment on my credit card after all this month.*

Carrie berated herself up for asking Mark to dinner, letting him choose the restaurant, and saying she'd pick up the bill. But it wasn't the first time that had happened to her. Somehow, she was sure she gave off a "screw me over" vibe.

Step 3 Tool—Relationship Resume

In Carrie's case, she was well aware of behaviors she had learned from her family and their cultural and religious beliefs. Fortunately, most of my clients already know they've been playing a large role in their dating struggles. Their biggest stressor is not knowing what to do or how to change their unhealthy habits so they stop doing them.

To begin with, I ask clients to provide me with their relationship history. But not just a quick list that they jot down on a notepad. Rather, I have them create a Relationship Resume. Similar to a job resume, a Relationship Resume is a chronological listing, with the most recent date or relationship listed first, and then all the previous men back as far as they can come up with.

This assignment tends to initially result in curious eyebrow raises and then some smirks as my clients begin to cycle through their past dates in their minds. Sometimes there's embarrassment if they think their dating history is too long or too short. I assure them it doesn't matter and that there is a point to this homework assignment.

For each name listed on your Relationship Resume, include:

- Length of the relationship (days, weeks, months or years) and the approximate dates when it started and ended.
- Did you have sex, and if so how soon?
- Who ended the dating/relationship, and why?
- Do you still have a connection or friendship with this person. If so, explain.
- A brief back-story of each individual—marital status (for example, single and never married, or divorced and their total number of marriages), family of origin, job/employment status, hobbies, and any other key factors, such as whether they have kids, if they travel for work, if they live nearby or a distance away, etc.
- And, a list of twelve positives *and* twelve negatives about each person listed.

It typically takes about a week to go back through your full relationship history and do this.

I invite you to initially jot down everything you can remember, and then set it aside for a while. What you'll likely discover is while you are busy doing other things your mind may still be mining the deepest recesses of your memory for more details. So keep a notepad handy for when something pops into your head, so you can quickly jot it down to add to your Relationship Resume. Feel free to tap into the memory banks of your trusted family and friends, as well, to see what they remember about your dating history.

Once it's complete and typed up, I have clients email it to me so I can review it in advance of our next session. If you're doing this on your own, you can share it with a trusted friend to help you identify patterns in your relationship history.

The Big Reveal

After Carrie completed her Relationship Resume, we hopped on a call to talk through it. She shared that it had been a bit unnerving at first to put down on paper all of her past relationships. There were a few that she admitted she didn't have a lot of information about, simply because she hadn't know those guys long enough, which is completely understandable.

From there, we looked at the pros and cons she'd listed for each, and I asked Carrie to tell me if she noticed any common themes or patterns in the men she'd listed. She paused for a moment, scanning her paper, and quickly said they were all jerks. I asked her to look deeper, to see what might be some things that stuck out more often, beyond the superficial things. She looked again and noticed that a lot of them had been recently divorced. She kept reviewing her list and then said, "Oh my gosh. The majority of them had commitment issues, mommy issues, or anger issues."

Carrie began to see that the majority of the "bad" men she listed had glaring similarities, and she couldn't help but say, "I sorta knew those guys were bad, but I still kept at it, falling for the same unhealthy types." I instructed her to highlight all the cons in yellow, to indicate caution.

We moved on to discuss the qualities Carrie liked about each guy (the pros in her pros and cons lists). Much to her surprise, she realized she had been drawn to more superficial qualities, like if they were physically fit and had muscular arms. She was also a sucker for sexy blue eyes, tattoos, and men who drove expensive or flashy cars.

There were two men on Carrie's list who did not seem to match with the other "bad" guys, and she hadn't shared much about them. When I inquired further, she said they'd been really nice, but had also seemed "kind of boring or weird." I pressed on and asked Carrie to say more.

"Well, Bert…. Yeah, I just couldn't get over his name. It was a family name, but it didn't sound like a grown-up's name. Plus, he was shorter than me, and I'm not that tall. We went on a few dates, but I told him I only wanted to be friends. He was disappointed, but we stayed in touch for about a year, occasionally talking on the phone, until he got a new girlfriend."

I had Carrie write down "weird name" and "shorter than me" on her relationship resume and highlight them in yellow.

I asked about the next guy on the list, Ted. Carrie said he'd been super smart and very sweet, but had two younger daughters he had full custody of, which wasn't really an issue, but he was also continuously dealing with his mentally ill ex-wife. She wrote down "crazy ex-wife" and highlighted it in yellow, then said, "You know, he did buy me flowers a few times, and he enjoyed taking me out for nice dinners and doing fun things with me. Now that I think of it, one of my exes popped back into the picture around the same time Ted was asking if I was ready to take our relationship to the next level. I'd never been talked to like that before and I guess I freaked. The next day, I broke it off with Ted and said I wanted to get back together with my ex-boyfriend."

It was clear that Carrie could see now how Ted didn't qualify as one of the "bad" guys. Hearing herself say aloud how respectfully he'd treated her caught her by surprise.

Being able to see the forest instead of only the trees was a huge aha moment for Carrie.

Evaluating the Negatives

Depending on the circumstances or the individual, you could have an extensive list of mostly good or mostly bad relationships. Or, if you barely knew someone, you might have hardly anything. Whatever you put down is fine.

First, we'll focus our attention on the cons. Getting clear on what we don't want any longer helps in creating boundaries with others and ourselves so we don't step into a proverbial pile of dog poop again. Make a list of all the negatives qualities you wish to avoid in the future and title it "Red Flags & Deal-Breakers."

Look at your list of cons and as you do I invite you to look at them in a more objective manner. For example, pretend for a moment that you are your best friend. Let's say that the Relationship Resume and the cons list is your best friend's and not yours. Close your eyes and envision your best friend having experienced all these negative things with guys and now coming to you for advice.

What would you say to her?

Would you let her continue to be a doormat and settle for sub-par men? Or would you be respectfully honest and tell her how much it hurts to see her stuck in these same unhealthy relationship patterns, and that she deserves to treat herself better?

I suspect it's the latter.

Evaluating the Positives

When it was time to home in on the real pros, those aspects Carrie was truly hoping to get from the bad guys that they were unable to deliver on, I had her grab a blank sheet of paper and start writing down the behaviors that she appreciated in other men, besides the ones listed on her Relationship Resume—men she knew outside of dating, guy friends, gay friends, husbands or boyfriends of her friends or family members. What were the characteristics of the "good" guys she dated over the years. I also had her include the good qualities she admired in the "bad" guys.

As we talked through each entry, Carrie's tone shifted from her initial embarrassment of what seemed like a long list of failures, to feelings of relief and happiness for the clarity she was gaining about herself.

Compiling your Relationship Resume, along with identifying the negative patterns and considering the positive characteristics, will enable you to see more clearly what you want in a future relationship.

But, before that can happen, we need to dive into learning about the wisdom you already possess.

Chapter 5

Step 4: Wake up to Your Own Wisdom

Connecting to your inner wisdom starts with *knowing* that you're ready to make this change. It's not that your time of being single and dating different "bad boy" types was wrong. Much to the contrary. It's that you realize now that you've learned enough to know better. And when you know better, you tend to do better. Struggles and challenges continue to come to us until we've learned the hard, yet valuable lessons from those experiences.

When Michelle was in the middle of her relationship detox process, she disclosed that when she'd watched the movie, *Eat, Pray, Love* she'd had a major aha moment. She said, "I realized that all the men I had met and dated were teachers for me. They were teaching me all along what I didn't want and what I wasn't willing to settle for. There were some good things from those experiences, too, and I discovered interests I hadn't even known I had. So it wasn't all bad."

As Michelle discovered, her so-called "failed" relationships were all meant to happen in her life so she could better identify what she truly wanted in a future partner.

Creating Your Ideal Relationship

Your relationship detox journey begins with the end in mind. In this step, we take what you've learned so far and begin to formulate your ideal relationship partner. This involves getting serious about taking care of yourself.

Yes, some the steps may seem like a stretch or even a bit scary. If they weren't, you'd likely have done this sooner on your own.

Envisioning Your Future Life

I have a hunch you're familiar with vision boards and have maybe even made one for yourself—on Pinterest or by using poster board and magazine pictures. Vision boards are a great tool for capturing your dreams and wishes and setting the stage to manifest what you desire to have in your life.

If you have not created a vision board yet, I invite you to do so at this stage. Go to your local discount department store and buy some poster board, glue, and scissors. Then gather a variety of magazines—you can contact your dentist's office, primary care doctor or specialist to ask if you can have their old magazines. Most switch out their magazines weekly or biweekly.

Once you've got all your supplies handy, start going through the magazines and clipping out pictures, words, or phrases that resonate with you. Select them from a mindset of where you want your life to be, what you want it to look like, and how you want to feel. In doing so, your energy and attention will have a focal point to strive for. It's also about staying anchored to your power and saying, *I'm choosing this* and *I'm going to make this happen.*

If you prefer to create a digital vision board, you can do so by creating a relationship dream board on Pinterest. If you don't want others to see what you pin to that board, you can make it private. Digital boards may be convenient, but my clients have found them to be easy to forget about unless they print off their pins and glue them on a piece of poster board.

Become the Future You

A benefit of creating a vision board is that it begins to shift your mindset away from where you *were* to where you *want to be*. You have an idea of how you want your life to look and feel in the future.

Next up is stepping into *becoming* that person. Part of how to get there sooner is to begin to *behave like the future you*.

If you want to be a self-confident woman who easily attracts high-quality, emotionally available men, you need to shift your life—your actions, behaviors, and thoughts—to match your future life.

In order to make this transition to who you want to become, you will need to get very acquainted with who you are right now, so that you can identify where the gaps are. It begins with tuning in to yourself. Tuning in to yourself may be challenging, mainly because it involves getting still and slowing your life down, at least now and then, so that you can begin to pay more attention to what's going on in your mind.

Step 4 Tool—Start a Journal

During your relationship detox, I encourage you to keep a journal. You can simply purchase a notebook—ideally something you can easily keep on your nightstand or carry with you in your purse or tote bag. Write down your thoughts, how you feel (positive, negative, excited, fearful, or whatever), what you're grateful for, what's driving you crazy, and even what you're learning or discovering. This includes stating when you've noticed yourself giving your power away and where you let your attention get diverted to.

Ideally, journal daily—you can try doing it first thing in the morning, at mid-day, or right before going to sleep at night. Because *life happens*, and it's not always possible to do it every single day, commit to writing in your journal at least four or five times a week. Throughout the FORWARD Framework process you'll be reminded about keeping a journal.

Journals help you to reflect upon how far you've come in a short amount of time. If you're anything like my clients, you'll look back at your journal in six months or a year and be amazed at how much your life has changed for the better.

Increase Your Self-Care

Get More Rest—A key to becoming the *future you* is to make sure you're getting enough rest and downtime. When you're getting enough rest, you're setting yourself up for better peak performance at your job, being more present with your kids, and not falling prey to unwanted drama. When you make getting rest a priority, you are practicing self-care. Giving back to yourself helps you feel happier and content. Being rested enables your mind to function with more clarity.

If you're not able to consistently get seven to eight hours of sleep a night, when next you have the opportunity, let yourself take a power nap (20 to 45 minutes). Naps can help reduce stress, alleviate headaches, and give a much needed boost of energy. Give yourself permission to sneak in a nap during your lunch break, on your days off, weekends, and even on vacation. Making rest a priority means you're putting *you* first and taking care of yourself.

Proper Nutrition—Our ability to focus better and feel less stress can be controlled by consuming healthy food and beverages. Be sure to limit your intake of sugar, flour, caffeine, and alcohol. All of these greatly impact your digestion, mental acuity, and energy levels, and affect your ability to sleep or lose weight.

Decline Invitations—Another way to practice self-care is to say no to events or get-togethers that don't fill you with joy. When you receive an invitation, first give yourself time to think about it and check your schedule. You don't have to give an answer on the spot. Secondly, give yourself permission to say no.

Make excuses if you feel the need, but know that you don't owe anyone an explanation! Excuses are a way for us to spare the other person's feelings and hopefully hear from them that it's okay if we don't attend. However, simply saying "I'm not going to be able to make it" is an honest and empowering way to stay true to yourself.

Get a Massage—Massage, reflexology, cranial sacral, or reiki treatments can help you relax and let go of stress. Massages also offer many therapeutic benefits to health and are great for relieving muscle soreness from exercise, shortening illnesses, and help us focus better.

Tapping into the wisdom you already possess and implementing self-care will help you to become the *future you* sooner.

In the next chapter, we'll talk about how to let go of past behaviors and ways of thinking that you need someone else to make you feel whole.

Chapter 6

Step 5: Take Action

Before you can take action, it's important that you're realistic about what you can incorporate into your schedule and life, and that you create structure, or you'll risk setting yourself up for frustration. As you read on, I encourage you to select and incorporate activities that fill you up and, as you move forward, try swapping out activities to try, based on your interests.

Step 5 Tool—Adopt Healthy Transformative Alternatives
Healthy Transformative Alternatives (or HTAs) are activities you can include in your life that take the place of internal

drama and self-judgment. HTAs are *not* distractions, because distractions allow us to stay where we are and continue to lie to ourselves. Rather, HTAs will help you focus on yourself, allowing for clarity about what you want, as well as space so you can heal from past experiences. They are also a way to help build your self-confidence and explore new and exciting activities.

Practicing HTAs teaches you to anchor yourself and keeps you from sliding backward into old habits you want to change.

We spend so much of our lives in reaction mode and *giving* or *always doing* for others that we can get lost. We can forget that *we* are a priority in life too. HTAs fill voids of extra time and keep loneliness from creeping in.

As you adopt the HTAs that fit with you and your life, you'll begin to feel more empowered and self-confident.

As you read through the Healthy Transformative Alternatives below, jot down those that resonate most with you, even if, for now, it's more than three.

Spend Time with *You*

Spend time alone with yourself so that you can reconnect with and be *okay* with yourself. We expend a lot of energy when we're around other people, so spending some time alone is a great way to conserve energy and, in turn, honor your "me time," as well.

Intentionally schedule time alone into your day or week. That can take the form of doing something as simple as going for a walk, reading, or taking a nap. Even if it's a little scary, challenging yourself to be with *only* you will pay off big-time, so do practice it.

There are lots of things you can consider as me-time activities. You can go to a movie by yourself, browse through retail stores, explore museums or art galleries, take a drive to the local library or bookstore and find some interesting books to read, take up meditation, or spend some time in nature—at the park, take a hike, or visit a state park.

Work it Out

Exercise is an excellent way to make taking care of your health a priority. You're seeking love, right? So start with loving yourself. Exercise helps burn away stress, plus it offers a wonderful brain chemical mix-up that can give you more clarity.

Plan your workouts for when they work best for you (mornings before work, during lunch, in the evenings, or on the weekends). You can work out with friends or coworkers, or go by yourself and make new friends. It will also immerse you in a supportive community of like-minded people with similar health and fitness goals.

Workout facilities can sometimes seem like you're at an eye-candy buffet. Stay true to your Cleanse Commitment and be mindful of not falling prey to temptation.

Make a Difference

Get involved in your community or a cause, or become a volunteer. It's a great opportunity for you to focus your time and energy on helping others in a way that's not centered around unhealthy motives, such as people-pleasing or approval-seeking. Do it for yourself. Think of it as your chance to *pay it forward*. Getting involved in this way also helps you feel good about yourself—which is another thing we falsely think we're going to get from a relationship. The more positive and fulfilling activities you allow yourself to be a part of, the less room you have for the old habits, drama, or toxic people.

Get Creative

Our lives tend to be so packed full of work and to-dos that we can forget about the benefits of allowing ourselves time for being creative. When you're feeling creative, activities are more like play than work. You can discover new things about yourself, what you like and don't like, and what you want. Creativity allows for expansion in your mind—new ideas and ways of seeing things differently begin to emerge. Unleashing your creative side can be empowering and help rebuild your self-confidence.

Challenge Yourself

Challenging yourself is a great way to expand your experiences and try something new. This is your chance to take the lead and try something all on your own, just for yourself. You could start a side business, teach a class, take a class, or start an active hobby like cycling or kayaking.

Hit the Road

Take a daytrip, a weekend get-away, an extended weekend visit, or—better yet—a full-blown vacation to somewhere you've wanted to go. Go by yourself or with a friend or relative. It's a chance to experience new things that you haven't been able to do before, and it's a great opportunity to check off those dream destinations on your bucket list.

Or, if friends or family have been inviting you to come visit and you've always said you couldn't—whether they're states away or a few hours' drive away—guess what? No more excuses! Pack your bags, sweetheart. The change in environment, the chance for new adventures, and the fun company will do you good!

The Power of Pets

You're looking to give and receive love, right? A pet can help you along beautifully. One thing we miss when we're not in a relationship is having a place to put all this love we have to give. Consider getting a pet to give to and receive that unconditional love you've been looking for.

Pets provide companionship and help you feel more grounded and purposeful. They also require structure and attention. So instead of staying out all night at a party, you have a responsibility to come home and care for your pet.

Dogs, for example, need to get regular exercise—so it's a chance for you to also get some exercise at the same time. Go for a walk or run, check out the new hiking path, or venture through a new neighborhood. You can even take them to the local dog park to play with other canines.

Seek Out Support

Professional Help—Getting support is another way to love yourself. If you've been in a toxic relationship previously—or a series of them—then seeking help from a certified life coach will aid in your healing and recovery process. They can also be your accountability partner in helping you find your ideal relationship. These professionals are specifically trained to help you identify the underlying reasons and thought patterns that are keeping you stuck, and provide you with the tools and support that can help you swim out of that pool of despair, heal, move forward, and achieve your goals.

Support Network—Connect with people you admire. Reach out to family or friends who've been through similar experiences and who exude self-love. Do you know someone who has totally embraced their singleness? Who's confident—but not cocky about it—and knows they don't need anyone else, but is open to whatever happens next? Someone who's really good with being single? Do you know someone like that? If so, reach out to *that* type of person to hang out with and get to know better.

Or reach out to someone you know who *was* single and exudes self-love even after finding the relationship of their dreams. Reach out to *them*, because that's where you'll get some great support!

This transformation belongs to you! It's time to let go of past ways of thinking, embrace being single, and adopt Healthy Transformative Alternatives into your life.

In the next chapter we'll identify potential drama and challenges that can arise along your relationship detox journey.

Chapter 7

Step 6: Raise Your Resilience

The biggest things that come up with my clients who go through the FORWARD Framework process are *drama* and getting in their own way. Drama can show up in a variety of ways. Knowing what it can look like will help you see it more objectively, so that you can best manage it.

Being resilient when challenges arise is a key to keeping you on your path to success and finding your ideal relationship.

Fostering Resilience

Resilience enables you to perform at your best with your Cleanse Commitment and overall transformation. But it takes a lot of time and effort when you attempt to go at it by yourself. Until you unlock this skill set within yourself, your ability to become the *future you* will be weak. Until you realize your own resilience potential, you will not attract a man worthy of being in your life.

This exact mistake is what took me down many wrong paths, wasting time with unfit men. I got distracted. I broke my own Cleanse Commitment. I lied to others and I lied to myself. I let myself fall prey to believing the untruths said by the toxic men I had met—that there *must* have been something wrong with me and nobody could ever live up to my standards.

Then there's the other big fat lie: that all the *good men* are taken already.

I've come to realize that it was the resilience I was born with that got me out of my abusive first marriage and then out of a highly toxic rebound relationship—but I had forgotten it when it came to dating. That cost me staying stuck in a cycle of thinking I had to prove myself to a man and be a chameleon (liking what he liked or wanted) in hopes that he'd accept me.

What I learned after years of struggling is that I didn't have the right support or resources to foster my *resilience potential* so that I could truly step forward into the unknown and take bigger risks. When I remembered and reconnected with my resilience potential, I was able to look challenges in the eye, overcome them, and successfully complete my own relationship detox.

Step 6 Tool—Identify Your Drama Potential

Here's a list of common dramas that may arise. Familiarizing yourself with these will help you be more aware of ways you might be self-sabotaging your relationship detox process.

Waiting to Start—Waiting until everything in your life is perfect or finished before embarking on your relationship detox will more than likely turn into not ever starting. Similar to saying the diet will start *after* the holidays are over, waiting to start on a relationship detox will not change your current state.

Doing Too Much—If you think cramming all the HTAs into your life will make the process go faster... it won't. Instead, you've simply replaced your previous busyness of dating pursuits, chasing men, and being on the prowl with different busyness activities. Doing too much results in not allowing yourself to slow down so you can practice self-care.

Playing the Losing Game—What if you haven't *really* committed to the process and are still active on dating sites? What if you're pretending to be following the rules, but are keeping the back door open, just in case Mr. Wonderful shows up and rescues you from having to do actual work on yourself? Going on secret dates or trying to half-ass your relationship detox will only result in you *staying exactly where you are*. The truth is, if you don't have both feet in, you're afraid of being on your own, and that will spin into fearful thoughts around ending up being single forever.

Doubting the Process—As discussed in an earlier chapter, the FORWARD Framework process is not easy-peasy. It is hard work, but it is definitely worth it. You could be *all in* and nearing the half way mark and someone randomly says something upsetting and you find yourself flooded with fear. You worry if this will actually work for you or if you'll ever find your ideal relationship. Anytime you embark on a life-changing journey, it's important to *trust the process*. Fear is a natural instinct meant to protect us, but if you let it hang around, your fear will begin to sabotage your efforts.

Assume It's a Quick Fix—Going through your own relationship detox sounds all cool and great, at first, and you may feel really motivated and excited for your life to change.

But then, somewhere along the way, you get bored. The shininess has worn off and the reality of it being a process that takes time doesn't feel so fun anymore, and you want to give up on yourself.

Not Fitting In—There's a chance that, because of this new journey you're on and all of the changes you've made, you feel like you don't fit in with your friends anymore. Your single "on the prowl" friends may *not* be interested in meeting for lunch or going to a movie, because they'd rather have fun hanging out with you in the clubs. Or they may begin to look at your friendship differently, and feel inferior to you or think you're boring. *Boring* is a not-so-nice way to refer to contentment and being drama-free.

Trying to Do It All Perfectly—There is no perfect way to go through your relationship detox. Everyone's experience is unique and this program is designed to accommodate those various differences. Despite feeling empowered and optimistic, be careful not to expect or try to force your process to go perfectly, because it may not. When your focus is on doing it perfectly, you lose out on learning how to navigate change, and that can result in feeling ashamed or depressed.

The truth is, embracing being single helps to *open you up* to new opportunities and to getting to know yourself better.

Holding on to your former identity only keeps you all hyped up and anxious, or tuned in to needing to have consistent attention from men. In that case, you're measuring your self-worth by the amount of attention you garner.

In situations like those listed above, it's important to understand that you will not have the future success you so desperately want if you don't do the work needed to get there. If you don't actually *invest* in yourself by doing a relationship detox, the bad news is that the chances of getting the results you dream of will be bleak. You have to invest in your own results to be able to manifest your future ideal relationship.

Managing the Drama

Drama will come up at different times and in different ways, some of which are mentioned in this chapter. What's important is that if you find yourself stumbling or you get knocked off track, you don't have to give up or quit. Challenges arise to test your commitment to becoming the *future you* who will be ready to accept the relationship of her dreams.

We can choose to get sucked into the drama. We can decide to believe whatever story we tell ourselves, because we can find evidence to make *anything* seem true. But no matter what drama comes up, you have choices about what you believe, and you can lean into the FORWARD Framework process. When fear arises—and it most likely will—you will have to feel the fear and *keep moving forward anyway*.

Having an accountability partner, mentor, or coach is a great way to manage the drama when it comes up; plus, it's insurance that you will get the results you want for yourself.

Fostering resilience will help you better avoid *potential* drama and manage *unexpected* drama that may arise during your relationship detox process.

In the next chapter we'll discuss the final step in the FORWARD Framework process –how to maintain structure, develop a game plan, and establish boundaries to avoid sliding backwards.

Chapter 8

Step 7: Dedicate Yourself
to Your Success

I n earlier chapters, you learned about embracing being
single, practicing self-care, becoming the *future you*, and
adopting Healthy Transformative Alternatives (HTAs).
The cool thing about being at this point is that you've
already learned how to make many lasting changes in your
life—which is something so many others only dream of
doing for themselves.

Too often, women say they're going to wait until "this or
that" happens, or some date comes, or—worse—that they're
going to stay bitter toward men—while they secretly wish

and pray that he'll show up on their doorstep and sweep them away! Well, I can assure you that no Prince Charming is going to magically appear!

If you do the work, you're going to get the "keys to the kingdom" when it comes to becoming the *future you*. In this chapter, we gear up information to set you up for success.

Maintaining Structure

As you embark on your journey to becoming the *future you*, your chances of success are much greater if you lay out a game plan. Having the structure of a plan helps to prevent situations where you're saying, "What should I do today?" Or this evening or this weekend. And then you slide backward into old, unhealthy habits—because those you've already figured out, so they're familiar.

The concern of having a misstep and reverting back to bad habits is eradicated by having a game plan and a schedule, because you've decided in advance what you'll be doing. It prevents you from making excuses or skipping out on putting *you* first. Creating that structure keeps you from falling prey to reactive thoughts or emotion-based fears, because everything is already lined up and planned out.

The Unintentional Slip

Sarah's first attempt at a relationship detox didn't go so well, because she didn't have a plan of action, let alone any structure. She thought she'd just... wing it. After only a few days—when her kids were gone for an extended visit with their dad—she found herself feeling super lonely. She hadn't made any advance plans for the weekend, and her friends and family were all busy or out of town. Sarah had already forced herself through finishing all the household chores, and there was nothing interesting on TV. She couldn't think of any good movies to rent.

Sarah was bored, which soon turned into feeling lonely. She was flooded with doubts that she wasn't strong enough to do this like she initially thought, and that if she stopped looking for a man, even for a while, she might miss the chance of meeting her dream guy.

Sarah quickly succumbed to those fearful thoughts and decided to hop online to see if there were any potentials willing to chat. It had been only a week since she'd sworn off men and dating, and now there she was, surfing for attention and choosing an unhealthy distraction to keep herself from feeling the discomfort of changing.

Fortunately, the attention she got from a few men online ended up being *more of the same*: disrespectful, unhealthy, and toxic behaviors she desperately wanted to stay away from. When it finally occurred to her what she was doing, she let out an angry scream and slammed her laptop shut. That turned out to be a great lesson for her.

The next morning, Sarah made the conscious decision to *fully* embrace the Cleanse Commitment. She cancelled her online dating subscriptions and laid out her game plan. She vowed to not allow herself to slip again and started making a list of all the things she'd been wanting to do for herself and with her kids.

Sarah looked online and, within an hour, had a plan of action for the next twelve weeks laid out. Her calendar included: attending all of her kids' school and extra-curricular activities, attending exercise classes, going to fun work functions, checking out local community events and festivals, taking a weekly beginners' painting class, as well as going to a few performances at the local theater. She even joined a book club that her girlfriend had been begging her to join.

Sarah was thrilled to have fun and interesting activities to look forward to each week. As she filled herself up with healthy and fulfilling things to do, her doubts and fears came less and less, until they weren't even a blip on her radar anymore.

Sarah didn't initially realize that by *not* having a plan of action she was sabotaging herself. She didn't understand how deciding to wing it meant leaving the back door wide open for fear to come in and throw her quickly off course.

Step 7 Tool—Developing Your Game Plan

If you stumble along the way, like Sarah did, the challenge will be deciding whether you're going to get back up, forgive yourself, and finally lay out a game plan—or do what too many women do and give up, decide it's too hard. I'm writing these words to you today because *I* didn't totally give up on myself, even when the process got hard and I got scared.

Fear will still want to visit you along this journey, but you have the power to not allow it to consume you. You'll become the *future you* if you accept that fear will want to visit again, *and* you decide to do the work anyway.

Part of creating a game plan is to start making a list of those things you *want* to do—this includes a minimum of three things from the HTAs list. These can be things you go do by yourself, with your kids, or with emotionally healthy and supportive friends or family.

To see clearly what time you have available, you may wish to first block off things that are required or top priorities, such as your work schedule, dinner time, kids' activities and homework time (if applicable), exercise classes, or standing obligations such as family get-togethers, religious activities, holiday functions, etc. From there, start filling in the resulting calendar blank spots with additional fun activities and events that will help reduce the chance of you—especially in the beginning—having an unintentional slip because you have *too much* unplanned down time.

Regardless of whether you have a misstep, it'll be great experience to step back into the ring and taking back your power.

Establishing Boundaries

Embarking on your relationship detox journey can feel very exciting, and you can even have your game plan in motion and everything may be going great. But as you are stepping into your new routines and enjoying doing fun activities, there may be outsiders who don't fully understand what you're doing and why. They may try to test your commitment to your newly chosen lifestyle.

A few years ago, my client Tracy told me that she'd been noticing that some friends seemed insistent on inviting her to parties where single guys were attending. Her friends were playing matchmaker and trying to get her to meet their newly single, hot, male coworkers. They even forwarded emails showing *featured guys* from dating sites. At first, Tracy laughed it off, but as time went on it began to bother her more and more. She reminded her friends that she wasn't interested in dating, but they still persisted.

I queried Tracy on what, exactly, she had told her friends about her relationship detox. She'd told them she was taking a break from dating for a while, because she hadn't been having much luck and wanted to enjoy not trying to date so she could focus more on herself. She thought they'd understood what she meant, but instead they seemed to ramp up their efforts even more.

Tracy's intentions were good, but the problem was with the language she'd used. She hadn't been clear enough with her friends. She'd used wording that was too passive, so it sounded more to her friends like she was *asking* for help with finding a guy, because she'd said she "hadn't had much luck." Tracy's friends, unfortunately, hadn't discerned what she really meant.

Become the Alpha

One of the key things to consider when you're going through this FORWARD Framework process and thinking about who you want to become—that *future you*—is the language you use.

When Tracy shared with me the struggle she was having with her friends, we discussed how she'd initially approached the situation. It was apparent that she hadn't communicated with them from a place of confidence or in an assertive fashion. Rather, she was more passive and hoping they'd read between the lines, because she felt somewhat embarrassed about struggling with dating.

Part of becoming the *future you* involves shifting your language and adopting an alpha role when communicating with others. Now, this is not to be confused with aggressiveness or being a bitch about things, but rather using language that's self-respectful and assertive.

Let's say you're at the coffee shop and run into a former coworker you'd lost touch with over time. You two enjoy a few minutes chatting and she says, "We should get together for lunch and catch up." Instead of responding by saying, "Yeah, that'd be great. Shoot me a message on Facebook and we can set something up," which might lead to her urging you to go out to a club with her some evening, *you* take the initiative and tell her that you happen to be free next Wednesday for lunch and ask if that works for her. This eliminates internal questioning that could come up for you around your friend or what you will do together.

When Tracy and I discussed her taking on an alpha role, she quickly saw that her embarrassment was really fear of what her friends might think. She was nervous about going through the FORWARD Framework process, so she tried to pretend it wasn't a big deal. After Tracy practiced using *alpha language* during our session, she was ready to have a straight-forward conversation with her friends. She respectfully asked them to stop trying to help her find a guy, and instead support her during her transformation process.

Once Tracy confidently shared the full truth about what she was doing for herself and asked for what she wanted, things quickly changed for the better. Her friends dropped trying to be matchmakers and shifted their suggestions to doing fun things together, like going out for girls-only dinner and movie nights, getting their kids together for hang-outs, and going to fun kid- and family-friendly events that weren't centered around dating.

This is a very common issue that comes up, especially if you have friends or family who tend to want to be over-involved in your life, who are fearful of you being single, or even who have big hearts and can't resist the urge to help those they love be happy. They mean well, but if you don't establish boundaries with those individuals—either up front or when a situation happens—you may find yourself feeling unnecessary stress or being tempted to break your Cleanse Commitment.

Dedicating yourself to your success will help you build your self-confidence, and enable you to lay out a solid plan of action to help ensure a successful relationship detox.

In the next chapter you'll learn the true value of the relationship detox process.

Chapter 9

The New You

I've given you all of the tactics and strategies in the FORWARD Framework process, but my wish for you—what I really want—is for you to start becoming a leader in your own life—the *future you*. That starts with learning how to stand on your own and becoming your own *source* of strength, knowledge, and happiness (and, yes, that is within your power), instead of relying on a man to provide you with that.

Start to recognize that you're *doing this*. Don't just say you're *going to*, but actually commit to doing it and begin.

Commit to seeing yourself for who you really are: a confident woman who's smart, capable, and deserving.

Standing On Your Own

Finding your *source* of power comes from trusting in the process of the relationship detox, using the tactics and strategies provided, and learning how to think differently by practicing doing it. Thinking differently about yourself, your life, and what you truly want your future to look like is key. That gives you the opportunity to truly grow your self-confidence in such a way that you can't help but change.

Finding your source of power also includes changing the language you use. For example, being able to unapologetically say, "I'm choosing not to date for the next few months so I can finally do things I've been putting off that I've always wanted to do."

Here's the core of this book and the relationship detox: *You learn how to give yourself everything you've been looking for from a relationship.* In doing so, you become a woman who automatically does things in her life that she enjoys, that bring meaning to her life, and that helps her feel more connected and present in her life, and for her children and loved ones.

That empowered woman, your *future you*, is a lot more likely to find a relationship that really works for her.

Living the New You

There's nothing like the experience of actually being single to teach you about *how* to be single. You start to really learn how to tap into and trust your own internal source of happiness and contentment, and that transforms you into the *future you* sooner.

Robin could hardly wait to share with me that she was getting *really good* at being self-sufficient. She told me how great it felt to go and do the things she loved. All of her old obsessiveness of trying to find a man to fill that void she'd felt in her life was gone. She was finally able to reclaim who she truly was and create the life she'd always dreamed of. She was so proud of how she had been able to shift her perspective and, in doing so, open up a whole new realm of adventure and excitement for herself.

Your Ideal Relationship

The ideal relationship you crave is already there waiting for you to claim it. Connecting with it starts with improving your relationship with yourself. In that relationship, you want to feel safe to be yourself, you want to be treated well, and you want to feel self-confident. You want support and understanding, and someone to have your back.

You want a place to put your love.

My dear, all of those things already exist within you.

When you start with *you* and aim to become whole, your most amazing transformations will occur. You'll be poised for magical things to come your way.

Chapter 10

Next Steps

I have a pretty good hunch that, as you've gone through and completed the FORWARD Framework process, things have shifted for you. In order to identify what's changed, let's compare where you started with your circumstances now.

Where You Are Now

Reflect back on where you were and compare it to where you are today. Pull out your journal and look back at your past journal entries. Next, take some time to really feel into the questions below and use them to honestly assess where you are now. Go ahead and write out your answers to each of these questions:

- How are you feeling after these past few months of using the FORWARD Framework?
- What has changed?
- What has stayed the same?
- How much have you been structuring your time around yourself and your own priorities?
- What tugs do you feel to return to your old habits?
- How clear do you feel about who you are?
- How grounded and focused do you feel, and in what ways?
- What are aspects of your identity that you have rediscovered?
- In what ways have you put *you* at the center of your life?
- In what ways have you grown?
- What haven't you had the opportunity to do for yourself yet?
- What new goals, if any, do you want to set?
- Would you like more time to practice being the *new you*? Are you having fun focusing

on *you* and want to extend your relationship detox longer?

Your answers will reveal a great deal about the progress you've made. There are no right or wrong answers, nor is there a *right* speed at which to step into the new you. For some people it happens in a few short weeks, with help. For others, it can take a few years to do it on their own. Everyone's experience is unique. What I've discovered from my clients is that their transformation occurs *much* faster when they invest in themselves and engage an experienced coach or a group of friends in a similar situation, or a trusted mentor to walk alongside them and hold them accountable.

Moving Forward

Setting an intention to make changes in your life, committing to the FORWARD Framework process, and then actually doing the work will produce *amazing* results. You'll have more self-confidence; you'll know who you are, and you'll feel much more content with your life. In addition, you'll be able to begin to better assess what you truly want in a future relationship, because you'll have a newfound clarity.

In Chapter 4, you created your Relationship Resume and also made a list of the pros and cons for each relationship listed. The pros list contains characteristics you enjoyed and appreciated, and things you admired about each of your past relationships. The cons are the behaviors and aspects that you did *not* like and that you want to avoid as you go forward. There may even be things on your cons list that you feel are absolute deal-breakers.

Having done that deep dive into your past relationship history enables you to *now* look toward the future with fresh eyes. You may be a bit surprised or even somewhat embarrassed by how little you settled for in the past. That's the beauty of the FORWARD Framework process and the newfound clarity you possess now. As you look back now, you may realize even more things you do or don't want in a relationship. If there are new things you want to add to your lists, go ahead and jot them down.

Create Your Dream Relationship Profile

Creating your dream relationship entails focusing on things you want most from a future partner, starting with your pros list from your Relationship Resume.

Think about what things were missing in your past relationships. Jackie discovered during her relationship detox that it wasn't so much that her past relationships were all bad, but rather that they each were *missing* a key ingredient: having shared interests. She loved adventure and traveling to new places, but most of her past boyfriends weren't into that. Having that realization, Jackie added "likes adventure" and "likes to travel" to her list.

Once you have everything down that you want on your list, rewrite it (or type it out and print it) on a fresh sheet of paper and title it My Dream Relationship Partner Profile. Put your list up where you will be able to see it every day, such as on your bathroom mirror or your bedroom closet door. Having it in plain sight allows you to stay connected to that vision.

Envision Your Future Partner

As you focus on your Dream Relationship Partner Profile, tune in to how you *feel* as you read through it. How does being in that positive headspace feel? Do you feel lighter and more optimistic?

Envision yourself in a relationship with your dream partner and answer these questions:

- How are you carrying yourself?
- What does your life look like?
- What are you reading?
- What do you do in your free time?
- Imagine you're out for dinner together: What kind of drink do you order?
- What types of conversations do the two of you have? What topics do you discuss? What things do you share with one another? (Eavesdrop on one of those future conversations…. What do you hear?)
- What things do the two of you enjoy doing together?
- What else would you want for your life then?

Take some time to really imagine your future relationship and to anchor to it. Doing so will enable you to stay focused on what you truly want and deserve, and it will reduce the chance of you falling prey to another "bad boy" type.

Putting Yourself Out There Again

Based on what you've experienced in the past and what you know now, update your online dating profile. Remember to include any new hobbies you may have developed since you last had an active profile, and to update the specific criteria you're looking for.

When you get noticed or messaged, take your time in responding. Do your research. Does he fit with your Dream Relationship Partner Profile? If not, simply ignore him and move on to the next interested potential candidate.

Be a selective, picky alpha about what you want.

Above all, don't settle!

Chapter 11

Recaps and Reminders

H ere we are at the conclusion of your relationship detox. We've walked through my story and those of a number of my clients. We discussed that taking a dating hiatus is a gift, not a loss, and we went through the detailed steps of the FORWARD Framework process. You learned how to plan and structure your schedule, what to expect along the way, and about stepping into the *future you*.

My wish for you is that this book has offered inspiration and provided answers to your questions (even to ones you may not have thought of before you started), has filled you with hope, and has given you the strength to find your ideal relationship so you can step into your amazing and exciting future.

Where I Am Today

As of the publishing date of this book, nearly ten years have passed since I embarked on my relationship detox journey. I am long recovered from the drama and settling for less than I deserved.

Because of all of the work I did to get myself out of that dating chaos, *I changed*. I changed enough to want more for myself and to understand a lot more about what makes a healthy relationship. I gave myself permission to embrace being single and to explore life. I focused on myself, and on my kids and their needs. I traveled, went to graduate school, built new friendships, and strengthened relationships with loved ones.

What I experienced post-divorce as I learned how to embrace being single was scary, but it taught me so many beneficial lessons. From that experience, I learned:

- **About myself**—how to trust my intuition and my strength; how my self-worth is not dependent on a man giving it to me; that I am smart, lovable, and loyal; and what my level of perseverance is.

- **About relationships**—what's healthy and what's unhealthy (including friends and family); and how not to allow fear to hold me back or dictate my dreams and happiness.

A few days after my fortieth birthday, ten years after I'd been divorced, I went on a blind date and met a man who would become my best friend and the love of my life, Dan. He had a spark about him that I couldn't forget, and he possessed *all* of the important things I had been looking for in a life partner. We were married on February 13, 2013, during a sunset ceremony on a beautiful beach in Hawaii.

Since I met Dan, he has been my beacon if ever I feel lost, my sounding board when I need to vent or want advice, my cheerleader who always encourages me, a rock supporting me as I continue to pursue my dreams, and he's a great friend to and a positive role model for my boys.

I went on to pursue my academic goal of earning a master's degree. I left corporate America and enjoyed teaching and training in colleges. Now I'm a Certified Life Coach specializing in relationships and helping to make a difference in other people's lives. I am so proud to have the ability to share my experience and to support other women through the empowering and life-changing process of relationship detox as a journey to their future selves.

Continue Your Journey With Me

As you've read this book, there may have been others who came to mind that you feel could also benefit from my story and my experience. I invite you to share this book with them.

I have a companion video that goes along with this book. You can head on over to www.relationshipdetox-book.com to sign up for it.

If you'd like an experienced companion to walk beside you on your relationship detox journey, you can apply for my Relationship Detox program. You can find details on my website at www.relationshipdetox-book.com

I wish you strength and hope, and send you love and light.

Acknowledgments

I want to start by thanking my entire family for always standing by me, even if they disagreed or didn't understand; for being open-minded; and for being willing to learn from my life experiences. I appreciate them for all the joy and great memories they help create when we're together.

Thanks to my parents and siblings for encouraging me to find myself and to look at the world through a bigger lens; for showing me, by example, how to step through my fears, trust the process, stand up for myself unapologetically, and not settle. Thanks to my dad, for all his unconditional love, and to my mom for always pushing me to learn and to advance myself.

I am grateful to all my dear friends who provided moral support during my post-divorce single years—they know who they are! Thanks also to my inner circle of friends who've watched me transform from caterpillar to butterfly multiple times over. I'm grateful for their continued kindness, love, and support.

I have a deep appreciation for my husband Dan and my boys, for their unconditional love and for teaching me new things every day about life, through their knowledge and experiences. Also, I appreciate and love them for being authentic and fun, and for supporting my passion of making a difference in the world.

Thank you to the entire crew at The Author Incubator for their professionalism, support, and belief in helping authors fulfill their dreams. A special thanks to Angela Lauria for always holding me to a higher standard and encouraging me to not hide when the work gets hard. Thanks to my managing editor, Grace Kerina, for all her support and suggestions, and especially for being my wordsmith—all while retaining *my* voice.

To the Morgan James Publishing team: Special thanks to David Hancock, CEO & Founder for believing in me and my message. To my Author Relations Manager, Margo Toulouse, thanks for making the process seamless and easy. Many more thanks to everyone else, but especially Jim Howard, Bethany Marshall, and Nickcole Watkins.

I am eternally grateful for the countless clients I've had the pleasure of coaching, who had the courage to face their fears and allow me to walk alongside them during their transformations.

About the Author

 Jodi Schuelke is a Certified Life Coach, best-selling author, successful entrepreneur, educator, speaker, and coach mentor. She specializes in helping women who are struggling with their relationships discover breakthroughs so they can experience more freedom and joy in their lives. She is passionate about helping women reclaim their strength, open up new ways of thinking, and listen to and trust their intuition so they can move on from relationships that are no longer serving

them and find the relationships of their dreams, the ones they truly deserve.

Jodi knows first-hand what being in unhealthy relationships looks like and has nearly three decades of first-hand experience: ten years spent trying to *fix* her emotionally abusive first marriage, going through a divorce, co-parenting, enduring a tumultuous rebound relationship and break-up, dating again in her late thirties, journeying to find her dream relationship, and getting married again.

Jodi has had the privilege to train and be mentored by some of the most noted coaches in the industry, and holds a Life Coach Certification from the Martha Beck Institute. She also has a master's degree in management and organizational behavior, with an emphasis in training and personal development. In addition to her individual and group coaching, Jodi uses her coaching skills in her role as an adjunct professor and corporate trainer, teaching courses in interpersonal communications, sales, change management, and leadership.

She lives in Wisconsin with her husband, her sons and stepchildren, and a fur-child, Echo the Siberian husky.

Thank You!

Hey, thanks for reading *Relationship Detox*. This isn't the end, but rather the beginning of a life-changing and worthwhile future for you. I sincerely hope this book has provided you with peace of mind and encouragement as you prepare for your relationship detox.

I'd love to hear how *Relationship Detox* is changing your life. After you've read the book, post a thumbs-up selfie with the hashtag #ReadyForMyIdealRelationship and post it to Facebook or Instagram. You can tag me on Facebook at @ jodischuelkecoaching, or on Instagram at @jodi_schuelke_ life_coach.

Download the Free Video Class

I have a companion video that goes along with this book. You can head on over to www.relationshipdetox-book.com to sign up for it.

Start Your Relationship Detox

If you'd like an experienced companion to walk beside you on your relationship detox journey, you can apply for my Relationship Detox program. You will find details on my website at www.jodischuelke.com.

Vision Board Workshops

If you're interested in attending a Vision Board Workshop with me, visit my website at www.jodischuelke.com/workshops.

Morgan James
Speakers Group

www.TheMorganJamesSpeakersGroup.com

We connect Morgan James published
authors with live and online events
and audiences whom will benefit
from their expertise.

Morgan James makes all of our titles available through the Library for All Charity Organization.

www.LibraryForAll.org

Printed in the USA
CPSIA information can be obtained
at www.ICGtesting.com
JSHW021724180823
46817JS00002B/148

9 781683 505396